D1528975

CHOOSE YOUR OWN
CAREER
ADVENTURE

OLYMPICS

K. C. Kelley

Created and produced by
Bright Futures Press, Cary, North Carolina
www.brightfuturespress.com

Published by
Cherry Lake Publishing, Ann Arbor, Michigan
www.cherrylakepublishing.com

Photo Credits: cover, Shutterstock/lazyllama; page 5, Shutterstock/kizirsky; page 5, Shutterstock/the wada1976; page 5, Shutterstock/Marish; page 7, Shutterstock/raindrop; page 8, Shutterstock/Maksim M; page 9, Shutterstock/Galina Barskaya; page 9, Shutterstock/ksstvdija; page 11, Shutterstock/ITALO; page 13, Shutterstock/Michael Pettigrew; page 13, Shutterstock/Lindsay Douglas; page 15, Shutterstock/Fotokvadrat; page 17, Shutterstock/MO_SES Premium; page 17, Shutterstock/topseller; page 19, Shutterstock/lazyllama; page 21, Shutterstock/Csaba Peterdi; page 21, Shutterstock/PhotoSerg; page 23, Shutterstock/Peter Bernik; page 25, Shutterstock/wavebreakmedia; page 25, Shutterstock/Café Racer; page 27, Shutterstock/Rawpixel.com; page 29, Shutterstock/Rocksweeper; page 29; Shutterstock/Pete Saloutos.

Library of Congress Cataloging-in-Publication Date

CIP has been filed and is available at catalog.loc.gov.

Printed in the United States of America.

OLYMPICS

Let the Games Begin!

Every two years, the best athletes in the world gather to take part in the Olympic Games. They ski, skate, sled, and more in the Winter Games. They run, swim, ride, and even more in the Summer Games. Athletes have trained for years for this big moment, and the eyes of the world will be upon them.

The Olympic Games are the biggest sports events in the world! Big events need lots of people to run them. The athletes may get all the glory, but thousands of **professionals** work for years to make those golden moments happen too.

Each nation that sends a team to the Olympics needs people to organize that team. Each **venue** where the athletes will play needs someone to run it. Someone must make sure the setting looks dazzling! Other people **volunteer** their time to make sure the host city looks beautiful too.

Just because some Olympics jobs don't get a **gold medal** doesn't mean they're not vital. Whether you plan to sweat on or off the playing field, it's time for the Games to begin!

TABLE OF CONTENTS

GRAPHIC DESIGNER

Like art? Like sports? **Graphic designer** needed to create the winning "look" for the Olympics. Includes making signs, designing costumes and uniforms, creating the **logo**, and choosing the **mascot**. The perfect **candidate** is super creative, knows the latest computer design programs, and is able to accept **constructive criticism** from lots of people.

- *Ready to take on this challenge?*
  Turn to page 6.

- *Want to explore a career as a Gymnast instead?*
  Go to page 9.

- *Rather consider other choices?*
  Return to page 4.

Go behind the scenes with the designers of the London Olympics at **http://bit.ly/London OlympicsBranding.**

The Olympic Brand

The athletes will do the running, but they run wearing your clothes. The fans buy the tickets, but those tickets have your fingerprints on them. You don't run the **arena** or the **stadium**, but all the decorations came from your creative mind. Look around. This Olympics could not have happened without the graphic designer—you!

Logos and Colors and Flags—Oh My!

Your most visible symbol of the Olympics is the **logo** you created. This colorful, eye-catching, and symbolic mark is just about everywhere. You came up with the design first. Then you had to present it to dozens of people, including the **U.S. Olympic Committee**. You made some changes here and there until it was finally approved. It will be part of Olympics history forever!

When an Olympics comes to town, the entire city is blanketed with color. Your job was to choose those colors and put them to work. You designed banners to hang from light poles all over the city. The flags flying at the stadium, the signs surrounding the field, even the name tags worn by the volunteers—you had to make sure they all worked together. The key to a great Olympic design is to make everything look like it is part of one "family" of colors and looks.

At the same time, you had to be creative. Not every wall or stadium or person is exactly the same. A flag is different than a jacket or warm-up suit. So a lot of your time in the months before the Games was spent taking your main design and adjusting it to work in different ways and formats. You logo is so unique it looks good on everything!

The Mascot

Each host city designs a mascot to symbolize the Games and the city or country itself. In 2000, Sydney, Australia, had five different native animals as mascots. In 2006, Turin, Italy, created a sort of living snowball. In 2016, a creation called Vinicius—a mix of many Brazilian animals—represented the Games in Rio de Janeiro. Now it's your turn. What will you come up with?

You know that creating the mascot means getting approval from many people. Along with being creative, you have to sell your vision. In the end, you are very pleased with what you came up with.

Your Graphic Design Career Adventure Starts Here!

EXPLORE IT!

With your sketchbook handy, visit the Internet to find

The mascot designs for the past three Olympics

Pictures of the decorations at some past Olympics

A color wheel showing how different colors work best together

TRY IT!

Be Logo-rific!

Every Olympics has a logo. Pretend your home city is hosting the Games and design its logo. Use colors and symbols related to your area. Create a couple and have your friends pick the winner!

Time for Fashion

During the festive opening ceremonies, each team wears a special costume representing its country. The designs use traditional styles, colors, and outfits from that country's history. Choose a country and then combine your graphic sense with some fashion research to create a complete look for that country's team!

GYMNAST

Superstar **gymnast** needed to lead U.S. team to glory at the Summer Olympics. Well-trained, amazingly fit and flexible required. Courageous and creative are must-have qualities. Comfortable under pressure and not afraid of large crowds. Athletic ability and stamina vital. Huge smile and winning personality a plus!

- *Ready to take on this challenge?*
  Turn to page 10.

- *Want to explore a career as a Hockey Player instead?*
  Go to page 13.

- *Rather consider other choices?*
  Return to page 4.

Meet the stars of the U.S. gymnastics team at **https://usagym.org**.

To the Village!

Congratulations—you have made it to the Olympics as a **gymnast**! To reach the host city, you flew with the rest of your team to the site of the Summer Games. You settle in to the Olympic Village, where the athletes live. You have fun meeting people from around the world. And you notice that everyone is collecting little country-themed pins as souvenirs—and for trading. You brought some too and enjoy passing them around. But soon it's time to get serious. It's time for your event.

In the Arena

Wearing your official team warm-up gear, you march in with teams from around the world. The stands in the arena are packed. You see your flag waving and try not to get too emotional. This is the big moment, and you need to focus!

As a gymnast, you'll perform in several areas, one at a time. The scores from each area will be added up. The gymnasts with the highest totals earn the coveted medals. The women perform on the balance beam, on the vault, on the uneven **parallel** bars, and in the floor exercises. The men do the vault, floor exercises, and parallel bars too, but they also compete on the rings, the single bar, and the difficult pommel horse.

One after the other, you take on each challenge. You flip, jump, leap, and swing. You use your strength and your amazing flexibility to defy gravity over and over. Somehow, you do these super athletic feats with style and grace!

A Finish to Remember

Your last exercise is the floor exercise. You need a big score to move to the top of the standings. The music starts and off you go. Back and forth across the mat you tumble, doing splits, cartwheels, somersaults, and flips. You try to "stick" each landing, which means that your feet stay right where they land when you hit the mat. You finish with a flourish, giving the judges a big smile.

As you wait on the sidelines to see your scores, you feel confident that you game it all you got. If the wild applause from the audience is any indication, you really connected with them and charmed them with your energetic performance. It seems like forever but...

A few moments later, here come the tears. You have the most points—and you've won the gold medal!

Your Gymnastics Career Adventure Starts Here

EXPLORE IT!

Use your Internet skills to find out

The last five gold medalists in the all-around event

The names of five gymnastics moves

The story of the first Olympic gymnastics champion

TRY IT!

What's in a Name?

Many gymnastics moves have interesting or complicated names. Make a list of 10 specific moves that a gymnast makes. Which ones were named after a person?

Gymnast or Dancer

Some gymnastics events are done to music. Pick some songs and make up dances that have some gymnastics moves. Even practice will be fun!

ICE HOCKEY PLAYER

Ice **hockey player** wanted to compete in the Winter Olympics with the U.S. team. Superstar-quality skater, in great shape, and not afraid of contact. Comfortable as part of a team and ready to work hard. Ideal candidate will have great vision on the ice, understand every part of the game, and be ready to sweat for his country! Full set of teeth optional.

- *Ready to take on this challenge?*
  Turn to page 14.

- *Want to explore a career as a National Team Director instead?*
  Go to page 17.

- *Rather consider other choices?*
  Return to page 4.

Watch the greatest upset in Olympic sports history at **http://bit.ly/UShockeywin**.

Before the Action

Ice hockey is played on an ice rink with five skaters and one goalie on each team. One of those **hockey players** is you. At the Winter Olympics, you're part of your nation's hockey team. The first thing you get to do is take part in the opening ceremonies. At every Olympics, this big event is held to kick off the two weeks of competitions. Nation by nation, the athletes march into the main stadium or arena. You put on your country's unique costume and walk in, waving a mini flag! The cheers of the crowd fill your ears as you walk beside your teammates. In the days ahead, you will make sure they can depend on you.

On the Ice

Olympic hockey teams play several games in the first round. The teams that do the best move on to the playoffs, which lead to the gold-medal game. Before your team's first game, you finish putting on your gear. You lace up your special hockey skates, which are much different than the ones the figure skaters will use at the arena tomorrow. You strap on your helmet and join your teammates in front of the coach. He gives you a pep talk about the importance of teamwork. You look with pride at the national colors on your team's uniforms.

Teamwork

Hockey can't be played alone. Every member of the team has to give it his all, 100 percent of the time. A split-second mistake can cost your team a win—or the gold. Even as the puck speeds by, players change in and out of the game. You need to be ready for the coach's instructions to jump in and take your turn. You play a "shift" of 90 to 120 seconds, and then you need a breather. Hockey is very hard work!

You play well and score several goals. Your team is heading toward the ultimate showdown: the championship game.

The arena is packed with screaming fans. Millions more are watching on TV. The opposing national team desperately wants to win, but so do you. Back and forth the game goes. First, you fall behind. Then, you rally back. With less than a minute to go, the score is tied. You see a break, call for the puck, and fire a shot. Goooooaaallll! You've done it! Your team has won the gold medal.

Your Hockey Player Career Adventure Starts Here

EXPLORE IT!

Hit the Internet to find out

The nation with the most gold medals in ice hockey

The names of current National Hockey League players who have appeared in the Olympics

Five words of hockey slang that you did not know

TRY IT!

Ice Time

Time to learn more about hockey. Find a hockey rule book or an online site (such as www.nhl.com). Look up what these terms mean: blue line, red line, defenseman, faceoff, and crease.

A Different Game

This one is a little trickier. There are a few differences between ice hockey in the Olympics and ice hockey in the National Hockey League. See if you can find a list of those differences. How do you think they make the game different? Do you think it's hard for players to learn both sets of rules?

NATIONAL TEAM DIRECTOR

Explore some of the jobs offered by the U.S. Olympic Committee at **www.teamusa.org/ careers**.

Organized, inspiring, and creative person needed to lead a U.S. Olympics team. Sports-savvy, business expert required. Sales, design, and security experience preferred. International work experience a plus. Fluency in more than one language a plus. Frequent travel and long hours expected.

- *Ready to take on this challenge?*
  Turn to page 18.

- *Want to explore a career as a Venue Director instead?*
  Go to page 21.

- *Rather consider other choices?*
  Return to page 4.

Many Hats

Nearly 200 nations around the world have Olympic teams. And every one of them needs a leader. For your country, that's you!

Being a **national team director** is not a **9-to-5** job. You're busy from sunup to sundown getting ready for the Games. Once they begin, you're on duty 24 hours a day.

A lot of the job is planning. You plan how your athletes will travel to the site of the Games, and you work with local officials there. You plan for how all the gear will be sent—athletes need lots of stuff, from balls and sticks and uniforms to tape, ice, and special food. (You might even hire a chef to make your country's native food so the athletes feel at home.) Of course, you have hired a staff of experts to help you, but in the end, you're responsible for everything. Or, as President Harry Truman was fond of saying, the buck stops with you.

You're the troubleshooter. When anything goes wrong, it lands on your desk. A field hockey player gets lost? You get the call. A swimming coach is mad about his practice times? You get that call. A **VIP** didn't get the tickets she wants? You'll hear about it! And in every case, you remain calm and find a solution.

Ready for Anything

A big part of your work is meeting with the **media**. People back in your country want to know everything about the athletes. It's your job to make sure they hear the good news. And when something goes wrong, you'll get a call from the media about that too!

You also represent your country at the Games, so you always have to be polite and well-dressed. And you have to be ready for anything. You might just had a meeting with the cycling team that was complaining about a hot track, but your next visit is with a king. Ready for anything, that's your motto!

The Payoff

Bring a handkerchief. You'll need it when your athlete wins a gold medal and your national anthem is played. You know you had a key part in making that happen, even if you didn't throw a ball or run the race.

Of course, not all your athletes will come home with medals. In those cases, you have to make sure they have a gold-medal Olympic experience anyway.

Your National Team Director Career Adventure Starts Here

EXPLORE IT!

Dive into the Internet and see if you can find

A list of all the nations that send teams to the Summer Olympics

The name of the director of the U.S. team at the 2016 Games in Rio de Janeiro

The name of the man who created the modern Olympics back in 1896

TRY IT!

A Very Busy Day

Imagine that your class is going to a day at the Olympics. See how many events you can attend in one day. You'll have to figure out how long each sport takes to play and if you can see more than one event at a single place. For example, a water polo game lasts about an hour, while a soccer match takes two hours. Go online to find real Olympic event schedules to help plan your day.

Foreign Affairs

Choose a country other than America and pretend to be its national team director. Go online to find out more about the country. What challenges would you face when leading that nation? How many athletes usually attend the Olympics from there? What sports will they do best at?

VENUE DIRECTOR

Super-organized leader needed to make sure events at an Olympic arena or stadium go off perfectly. Needs to know about sports, architecture, food service, **accounting,** and everything related to hosting huge international events. Should be good at directing many people at once, all while keeping a cool head.

- *Ready to take on this challenge?* Turn to page 22.

- *Want to explore a career as a Volunteer Director instead?* Go to page 25.

- *Rather consider other choices?* Return to page 4.

Meet the people who ran the 2016 Summer Games in Brazil at www.rio2016.com/en/ organising-committee.

Prepare to Juggle!

Putting on the Olympics requires having lots of places to hold competitions. Cities have to provide arenas, **stadiums**, pools, cycling tracks (called **velodromes)**, and horse-riding trails. Winter Olympics cities need **ski runs**, **bobsled tracks**, and **speed-skating ovals**. Your job as **venue director**? Running the track and field stadium at this year's Summer Olympics!

The security guard opens the gate to the stadium for you just as dawn is breaking. In a few hours, more than 100,000 people will be coming to your "house" for a track meet. You've got to make sure the place is ready.

Ready, Set, Go

As the director of the whole building, you have a lot of responsibility. First, there is the building itself. You meet with experts who have checked it thoroughly to make sure it is safe and ready. It turns out that some seats have to be replaced and one of the air conditioners is not working. There's also an electrical problem in a locker room. "Get those fixed . . . now," you say firmly, but with a smile!

Next, you meet with your food people. Spectators are going to want to eat and drink during the day, so you make sure that everything is ready for them. Did the ice truck arrive? What about the fancy food for the VIPs?

Nothing is more important than safety at the Olympics. You take a tour of the building with your security chief to make sure everything is ready: metal detectors, guard dogs, cameras, officers, and much more.

Open the Gates!

You've worked for many hours before the first fan arrives. Soon, the buzz of noise fills the huge stadium. Then, here come the athletes! The event begins. Race after race is run on the track. You barely get a second to watch, however. When problems come up, you have to solve them—and fast! This job calls for a cool head and a very organized mind. Of course, that's why they gave the job to you!

After the last medal has been awarded, the fans leave the stadium. More workers come in to clean up. After all, you have to do this all over again tomorrow!

Your Venue Director Career Adventure Starts Here

EXPLORE IT!

Do research online and find out

How many different places hosted events at the 2016 Summer Olympics in Brazil

Where the ancient Olympics were held

Which U.S. cities have been host to the Olympics (Summer and Winter)

TRY IT!

Hometown Olympics!

Pick a major city near you and make the argument that the Olympics should be held there. Why should they pick that city? What stadiums or arenas are already there? What else can visitors do in the city? How will they get around? Make your pitch for the Games!

Job Search

Turn on a big sporting event on TV—only don't watch the game! Instead, watch all the people working to make the event happen, from the food people and ticket takers to the security staff and scorekeepers. Write down all the jobs you see. In the Olympics, they'd all work for you!

VOLUNTEER DIRECTOR

Person to lead a huge crew of volunteers at the Olympics. Perfect blend of bossiness and diplomacy required. Must be able to use a radio, understand scheduling, and solve multiple problems at once. Nerve-wrecking pace with terrific job satisfaction guaranteed.

- **Ready to take on this challenge?**
  Turn to page 26.

- **Want to explore a career as a Graphic Designer instead?**
  Go to page 5.

- **Rather consider other choices?**
  Return to page 4.

Check out the volunteer packet for the 2016 Summer Games at **http://bit.ly/RIO2016Volunteers**.

Planning Ahead

Grab your clipboard and your radio and let's get to work. Being the **volunteer director** of an Olympics is a huge job. It's a good thing that you are very organized and know how stay calm in a crisis! Your co-workers say that you've never met a problem you couldn't solve.

Most of your work happened in the weeks and months before the Games. You met with the staff from every part of the Olympics to find out what kinds of **volunteers** are needed. At every venue, arena, and stadium, people will donate their time to help visitors. Some will give directions, while others might help with travel plans. Some work with the athletes at the Olympic Village. Others work at local airports or train stations to greet visitors. There is no shortage of work to be done.

The lists of volunteers needed grew with every meeting you had. Will you be able to find enough helpers?

Calling All Volunteers

You put ads on local websites and social media, as well as on radio and TV. "Would you like to be part of the Olympics? We need gold-medal volunteers to make sure our city hosts the perfect Games! Contact us if you want to be on the team!"

As responses start coming in, your staff sorts through all the **applications**. They match skills, such as languages or security, to jobs that need those skills. There are background checks to conduct and countless training sessions to host. Your job is so much easier when volunteers know what they are expected to do.

Let the Games Begin

As the two weeks of the Olympics begin, you are as ready! Good thing since every place you send volunteers, a problem comes up. A bus is late, a key volunteer gets sick, a **VIP** wants extra help. All those problems come to you to solve. But you're so organized, you have backup plans for your backup plans!

You don't see very much of the athletic action. But after all this hectic work is done, you can relax and watch it on video!

Your Volunteer Director Career Adventure Starts Here

EXPLORE IT!

Use the Internet and your detective skills to find

A volunteer application from a recent Olympics or from some other major sports event

A list of the volunteer jobs open at the 2016 Olympics in Brazil

A list of places you can volunteer in your community

TRY IT!

You Can Help

Are you a good organizer? Do you bake a mean chocolate chip cookie? Like to babysit? Make a list of the things you could offer as a volunteer. You can draw on these skills as a volunteer. Figure it out and volunteer for an organization you admire.

What Was It Like?

Many people who have given their time to volunteer have written about it. Go online and find three articles or blog posts by volunteers. One could be by someone who worked at an Olympics, one by someone at a hospital, and one by someone who works with children.

WRITE YOUR OWN CAREER ADVENTURE

WRITE YOUR OWN CAREER ADVENTURE

You just read about six awesome Olympics careers:

- Graphic designer
- Gymnast
- Ice hockey player
- National team director
- Venue director
- Volunteer director

Which is your favorite? Pick one, and imagine what it would be like to do that job. Now write your own career adventure!

_____

_____

_____

_____

_____

_____

_____

_____

Go online to download free activity sheets at www.cherrylakepublishing.com/activities.

ATTENTION, ADVENTURERS!
Please do NOT write in this book if it is not yours. Use a separate piece of paper.

GLOSSARY

9-to-5 slang term for a full day of work, from 9 a.m. to 5 p.m.

accounting keeping track of how money is made and spent inside a company or an organization

applications forms filled out to obtain a job

arena large indoor space used for sports events or concerts

candidate person who is being considered for a job

constructive criticism statements that show how something is wrong, but with an aim of making the work or project better

gold medal award given to the first place winner of an Olympic event

graphic designer person who creates the visual "look" for the Olympics and other events

gymnast person trained in the sport of gymnastics

hockey player one of six players on a team who competes on the ice by trying to score more goals than the opponent

logo graphic symbol of an event or a company

mascot animal, human, or imaginary creature used to represent a sports event such as the Olympics or a sports team

media broad term for anyone who works to communicate news to the public through TV, the radio, the Web, or newspapers

national team director person who leads a U.S. Olympics sports team

parallel lined up exactly opposite one another

professionals people who are paid to do a particular job

ski runs the long, snow-covered, downhill mountain paths on which skiing races are held

speed-skating ovals flat, ice-covered surfaces on which speed-skating races are held

stadium large building in which sports events are held, usually outdoors but can sometimes be enclosed

U.S. Olympic Committee national Olympic committee for the United States, founded in 1894 and headquartered in Colorado Springs

velodromes banked, oval, wood-covered tracks used for indoor cycling races

venue any place, site, or building that hosts a sporting event or concert

venue director person in charge of a particular building or site where Olympic events are held

VIP stands for Very Important Person, such as a government official, celebrity, or famous person

volunteer doing work without being paid, usually to help a good cause

volunteer director person in charge of making sure volunteers are placed where they are needed at an event

INDEX

ABOUT THE AUTHOR

K. C. Kelley has published dozens of books for young readers, mostly about sports. He is a former sports journalist who has written about the Summer and Winter Olympics, among other big sporting events.